SENSES

Sniffing and smelling

Author's Note

I have worked alongside young children for more than 40 years.
Over this period I have learned never to be surprised at their perceptive comments about the physical world in which they live. Many of their observations ('Have you seen the crinkles in the elephant's trunk?' 'How do seeds know which is their top and which is their bottom?') indicate keen observation and an intuitive use of the senses of taste, touch, sight, smell and hearing.

The sense-dependent nature of the young child should come as no surprise to parents and teachers. In the early years of life images provided by the senses shape our interpretation of our surroundings and lay the foundations upon which subsequent learning is built.
The ideas of hot and cold, far and near, quiet and loud, sweet and sour, soft and hard are developed through the interaction of the child with his or her immediate environment. This interaction encourages observation and questioning which in turn leads to talk and the extension and deepening of language.

This book (like its companions in the series) is a picture book which seeks to encourage both looking and talking. The text may be read by child or adult. Alternatively it may be ignored, the pictures alone being used to trigger an exploration of the child's own insights.

Paperback edition published 2000

© Franklin Watts 1997
Franklin Watts
96 Leonard Street
London EC2A 4XD

Franklin Watts Australia
14 Mars Road
Lane Cove
NSW 2066

ISBN: 0 7496 2574 0 (Hbk)
           0 7496 3789 7 (Pbk)

A CIP catalogue record for this book
is available from the British Library.

Dewey Decimal Classification Number: 612.8

Editor: Sarah Snashall
Art Director: Robert Walster
Designer: Kirstie Billingham

Printed in Malaysia

Picture credits

Commissioned photography by Steve Shott:
cover, 4, 5, 11, 21.
Researched photography: Bruce Coleman Ltd 14
(P. Clement), 18 (T. Buchholz), 27; Eye Ubiquitous 8-9
(D. Safhahevan); Images Colour Library 10;
Rex Features 29 (Mourlhion); Robert Harding 23
(Schmied), 31 (Kosel); Spectrum Colour Library 6-7,
17 (M. Birch); Tony Stone 12 (T. Craddock), 13
(P. Cade), 16 (P. Cade), 19 (R. Sutherland), 20
(A. Blake), 30 (S. Fellerman); Zefa 15, 24, 28.

SENSES

Sniffing and smelling

by Henry Pluckrose

FRANKLIN WATTS

LONDON • SYDNEY

4

When you breathe,
your nose helps you recognise
the smells and scents
which are carried in the air.

Some smells
are easy to recognise,
like the heavy smell
of smoke and fire.

Some smells are so exciting
that we can almost taste them,

like the mouth-watering smell
of fresh bread.

Some smells are sweet.
Does a banana, an apple
or an orange
taste like its smell?

There are many different scents
in the garden . . .
the clean smell of cut grass,
the tangy smell of mint,
the fragrance of roses.

The scents in a wood
change over the seasons . . .
in Autumn they are rich with
the musty smell of damp earth
and fallen leaves.

Farms have many smells . . .
the warm smell of living creatures,
the rich smell of ploughed earth,
the sweet smell
of harvested crops.

Along the coast the air smells
and tastes of salt.
In the harbour
even the boats seem to smell
of damp sand, salt and fish.

Not everybody
likes the same smells.
Do you like the smell
of cheese?
What about garlic?

Not all smells are pleasant.
Rush hour brings traffic to a halt.
The air is heavy
with the fumes of cars,
lorries and buses.
Breathing becomes difficult.
The air smells bad.

Our sense of smell
tells us about the world
in which we live.
A polluted river
has a sickly smell.
It reminds us that we must
care for the environment.

Animals have a sense of smell.
A mother sheep recognises
her lamb by its smell.
Her lamb has a different scent
from all the others in the flock.

Most dogs have
a very keen sense of smell.

Sniffer dogs are used to help the police.

We have a sense of smell,
but we smell too.
What things do you use
to make you smell sweeter?

Investigations

This book has been prepared to encourage the young user to think about the sense of smell and the way in which the nose interprets the multitude of 'scents' which hang in the air we breathe.

Each picture spread creates an opportunity for talk. Sharing talk with a sympathetic adult plays an important part in the development of a child's understanding of the world. Through the subtlety of language, ideas are formed, questioned and developed.

The theme of smell might be explored through questions like these:

* The nature of smell. What do we mean by smell? Are there some smells which you immediately recognise? Which smell do you recognise most easily? What do you 'see in your mind' when you sniff a familiar smell?

* Smells pleasant, smells unpleasant (pp 6-9, 20-21). Which things do you like to smell – or like smelling least of all? Does everybody (in your family/class) find the same smells attractive?

* Defining smell (pp 12-17). What words can we use to define a smell? What do we mean by a 'heavy' smell, a 'sweet' smell, a 'sour' smell? Can a smell be described as hot, cold, damp, dry – or warm? Can a smell be frightening or comforting?

* Messages from smells (pp 22-25). The way in which we live often pollutes our environment. The unpleasantness of some smells (like car exhaust) provides a warning of how careful we must be to maintain the quality of the air we breathe. What problems are caused when the air becomes too heavily polluted? How does air pollution affect health?

* Unity of the senses (pp 8-9, 18-19). It is important to talk about the way our senses work in harmony. What things can we identify simply through the sense of smell?

* The world of nature (pp 26-29). Like us, animals possess a sense of smell. Watch a dog or a cat. On what occasions can you *see* a domestic pet using the sense of smell?